# Lady Bird Johnson:
## Deeds Not Words

D1611931

**Louann Atkins Temple**

First published by Dog Ear Publishing
4010 W. 86th Street, Ste H
Indianapolis, IN 46268
www.dogearpublishing.net

ISBN: 978-1-4575-2409-7

This book is printed on acid-free paper.

Printed in the United States of America

to
Larry, with love

# *Table of Contents*

**Introduction**

**Part I:  Life Before the White House**

**Part II:  Life in the White House**

**Part III:  Life After the White House**

**Bibliography**

# Acknowledgments

The guidance of Mark Updegrove, the assiduous work of Jennifer Parks, and the cover design by Balmore Lazo created a book that shines for me.

The careful reading of Andy Bacon, Jo Anne Boykin, Shirley James, Harry Middleton, and Larry Temple made me trust my prose.

Thank you all for carrying me through the process. You made this book what I dreamed it could be.

# Introduction

Lady Bird Johnson was born just after the nineteenth century, a time when women played almost no role in the affairs of the world. She lived through the twentieth-century transition in women's lives and evolved into a twenty-first-century woman of action and influence. She said, on becoming First Lady, that her role would "emerge in deeds not words." She accomplished much, and she faced each new challenge with courage, persistence, and the kindness born of her understanding that change is difficult.

This small, trim, modest woman with jet-black hair and a soft Southern voice was both a traditionalist and a forward thinker, a woman who could not lean in aggressively and would not fall back defensively, a woman who stood up straight to be counted among those who worked for good.

If LBJ—Lyndon Baines Johnson—blew through this country with the force of a tornado, the other LBJ—Lady Bird Johnson—embodied the warmth of a gentle breeze, and she, too, changed America. This is her story.

# PART I

# *Life Before the White House*

*Growing up rather alone, I took my delights in the gifts nature offered me daily...*

*I suppose the most broadening thing that ever happened to me was entering the University of Texas at age 17, which is a wonderful age. All the doors of the world were suddenly swung open to me...a girl who had led a very narrow life.*

*...I did have several wonderful friends along the way who were determined to get me out of this business of being shy. And Lyndon of course was the vital steam engine.*

*My horizons have been broadening and my involvement getting deeper ever since.*

Lady Bird Johnson

# CHAPTER I

## *Growing Up*

Claudia Alta Taylor's life began in woodsy East Texas near the Louisiana border three days before Christmas, in 1912. Her father, Thomas Jefferson Taylor, was a big man, 6'2" and over 200 pounds, and strong enough to lift a 500-pound bale of hay; a successful man, who owned 65,000 acres of land, a general store, and a cotton gin; a man who was called "The Boss" or "Cap Taylor" around town. Her mother, considered sophisticated for that rural, remote corner of the state, was well-read and an opera lover. They and her brothers, Tommy and Tony, 11 and eight years older, called their home the Brick House. It had been built by slave labor before the Civil War. It sat on the edge of the town of Karnack and boasted 17 rooms, six fireplaces, and a circular stairway. Life seemed safe and good for this little girl, nicknamed Lady Bird, until one terrible day her mother climbed the staircase, their collie dog ran in front of her, she tripped and tumbled down the stairs, and a few days later, died. Lady Bird was five years old. At first, the child, not understanding death, thought her mother would return, but years passed, and she was left with scant memories of a woman who often wore white dresses and went around the house in a great rush and who read Greek myths and fairy tales to her.

4

Her father struggled to find a way to care for his little girl without a mother. (Tommy and Tony were away at boarding school most of the year.) For several months he took her with him to his general store, and when he had to work late, they even slept there. Then, he tried what he thought would be a better solution for her. He put her on a train and sent her to Alabama, where she had grandparents and uncles and aunts and cousins to care for her. But she and her father did not have each other, so Lady Bird's Aunt Effie Patillo, who was her mother's unmarried younger sister, returned to Karnack with the child to the Brick House and remained there until Lady Bird was grown. Aunt Effie loved Lady Bird and Lady Bird loved her in return, but Effie had health problems and was frequently sick. She never disciplined her niece or gave her advice or taught her how to dress. Sometimes, the child Lady Bird took care of the adult Effie, and in some ways the child reared herself. Often left on her own, Lady Bird wandered in the Piney Woods near their house, watched dogwood trees blossom out in the spring, picked wildflowers in the fields, spied turtles and snakes and alligators in shadowy Lake Caddo, heard owls hooting in the cypress trees, and developed a love of nature that never left her. As an adult, she remembered that "Nature was my first and most reliable companion."

She started school. Several times during her school years she tried to get her classmates to call her "Claudia" instead of "Lady Bird," but the nickname stuck. It had been given her as a small child by two of her black playmates, who, in turn, called themselves "Stuff" and "Doodlebug."

School consisted of one room and a single teacher for grades one through seven. Rarely did more than eight children attend, and one semester, Lady Bird was the only student.

A potbellied stove stood in the middle of the little schoolhouse, and on cold days, the boys brought in wood to start a fire. On Fridays, the children sang patriotic songs and quoted poems they had memorized. On Sundays, Lady Bird attended the Methodist Church, and in her free time, when she wasn't exploring nature on horseback or on foot, she read and cut out paper dolls. In the summertime she and Aunt Effie visited kinfolk in Alabama, where she hungrily absorbed family stories about her grandmother, who outlived four husbands and had 13 children, and her father, a farm boy, who rode a horse to Texas to make his fortune, but who returned to Alabama to convince Minnie Lee Patillo to marry him and come West, too. For many years, through many moves, Lady Bird carried with her a little box of letters her father had written her mother during their courtship. Family was all-important to her.

At 11, Lady Bird was propelled into a bigger world when she went to school in nearby Jefferson with dozens of boys and girls. Until then, she had been mostly with adults. Here, for the first time, she went to parties, where she watched the older girls dance the Charleston and rode—and crashed—a bicycle. For the first time, she had girlfriends to spend the night and play card games like Parcheesi and Old Maid. Then, at 13, her life expanded further when her father bought her a Buick and allowed her to drive alone to a high school big enough to support a football team, in Marshall, 13 miles away. She wrote for the school paper *The Parrot* and made good grades, but her shyness overwhelmed her in the face of so many new people. She remembered that when the captain of the football team "would come in and sit down by me and ask me about our assignment and this, that, and the other, I would make some excuse to leave or go out and get a drink of water simply because I couldn't think of what to say next." At graduation she was relieved to be third in her class rather than valedictorian or salutatorian, because those two students would speak at graduation, and "I would just as soon have the smallpox as open my mouth." Her solitary childhood had not prepared her for the teenage world of boys and speaking up in public. Shyness plagued her most of her life.

Lady Bird graduated from high school when she was 15, and for the next two years her world expanded intellectually while remaining confined socially. She convinced her father to let her go to a two-year college, the Episcopal St. Mary's College for Girls, in Dallas. There she lived in a dormitory, formed lifelong friendships, and became interested in the Episcopal church, in which she was confirmed a few years later. But she rarely saw boys, the girls wore uniforms, chaperones accompanied them when they went out, and the rules of behavior were strict. Aunt Effie often stayed in Dallas for weeks at a time and saw Lady Bird several times a week. At St. Mary's she developed two lifelong passions—for the English language and for theater. A half-a-century later she could still quote the English teacher who taught her to use words effectively: "Don't just say a man is cruel; walk him onto the stage and have him do a cruel thing. And be very sparse in the use of the verb 'to be.' Instead of saying, 'It was stormy,' saying, 'Thunder rolled across the heavens....'" Those lessons stayed with her, and all her life Lady Bird Johnson was known for her beautiful way with words.

Students at St. Mary's were taken to live theater performances at least six times a year and required to act in school plays. Lady Bird lost her shyness when she could hide behind a costume, makeup, and lines to read. It is hard to imagine this small, quiet, wide-eyed girl transformed into Shakespeare's raucous, fat Falstaff, but that was one of the roles she played. For the rest of her life, she delighted in attending the theater.

Then came four years at the University of Texas in Austin, a heady time for Lady Bird Taylor, in which she threw herself into the intellectual stimulation offered there, embraced a wide range of friends, and fell in love with the city of Austin. With 6,652 students, the university itself was 15 times larger than her home town of Karnack; men outnumbered women four to one; and the scenery included mesquite trees and cactus and limestone hills, so very different from lush East Texas. She was ready to take full advantage of this school and city.

The practical side of her demanded that she earn a teacher's certificate and take shorthand and typing so she could find a job after college. The intellectual side of her pursued history and philosophy. And the adventurous side sought a degree in journalism, because she had observed that journalists "were plunged into the happenings of the day" and "conversation around them was lively." As she had done in high school, she wrote for the school paper *The Daily Texan*. She studied hard and did well, graduating tenth in her class, in spite of squeaking by with a D in chemistry.

She lived in a boarding house with roommates who became good friends. Now she was feeling more confident and having a full social life that included picnics with beer, cheese, and crackers; horseback riding, at which she excelled; dancing, swimming, exploring a cavern by lantern light, or driving to Nuevo Laredo on the Mexican border. She never participated in organized sports, preferring just being outdoors. She went out with many young men but saw no one exclusively. Although she had no particular political leaning, she went frequently with a friend to the Capitol to watch the legislature in session, intrigued by the process and fascinated with the elaborate architecture of the building. She had a car and even found time to drive home 350 miles to Karnack to see her father about once a month. Life was expansive.

Soon after she graduated, while she still was in Austin, she met Lyndon Johnson, and her life changed fast and forever.

About 1915, Claudia Alta (Lady Bird) Taylor is two or three years old

Thomas Jefferson Taylor, Lady Bird's father, stands
on the front porch of the Brick House

Lady Bird with her Aunt Effie

Lady Bird in Karnack

Lady Bird graduates from the University of Texas

# CHAPTER II

## *Courtship and Wedding*

They met and married in 10 weeks' time. Such speed suited Lyndon Johnson's impetuous, decisive, always-in-a-hurry personality, but it ran contrary to Lady Bird's mindful, measured way of making decisions. He simply overwhelmed her. She was 21 and living in Austin. He was 26 and excelling at his job working for a congressman in Washington, DC. Now he felt ready to make the next commitment—to marriage. Almost immediately on meeting her, he decided Lady Bird was the woman for him. She, however, was still puzzling out her career ambitions. Should she teach, be a secretary, a newspaperwoman? She wanted to travel, perhaps work in Alaska or Hawaii, get married in the far-off future. In the meantime, she planned to go home to Karnack, remodel the Brick House for her father, and spend a year planning her next step.

Their first meeting was both planned and accidental. A mutual friend thought they would like each other, so when Lady Bird traveled to New York and Washington DC as a college graduation gift from her father, the friend gave her Lyndon's telephone number and suggested she call him while she was in Washington. Lady Bird, busy and having fun, never got around to making that call. Weeks later—on August 31, 1934—she dropped by to see this same friend at work in Austin just at the time that Lyndon, with a date, also came by the office for a visit. She later remembered, "He was excessively thin but very, very good looking, with lots of black, wavy hair and the most outspoken, straightforward, determined manner I had ever encountered. I knew I had met something remarkable, but I didn't quite know what." The very next day, at his invitation, they had breakfast together at the Driskill Hotel in downtown Austin. After breakfast he asked her to go for a drive with him. All day long they rode about the hills outside of Austin while he poured out the story of his life and his dreams for the future. He even confided his salary and how much insurance he had. He peppered her with questions about her own history and plans. Before the day was over he had asked her to marry him. Stunned, she replied, "You must be joking." He was not. They had only four days before he had to return to Washington, and he did not waste them. The next day the couple drove 30 miles to San Marcos, where Lyndon introduced Lady Bird to his parents. From there they traveled almost 200 miles to Corpus Christi for her to meet the congressman for whom he worked, followed by a 450-mile trek north to Karnack so she could present Lyndon to her father. Back in Washington, he called her or wrote to her every day, and he sent her his photograph, inscribed, "For Bird, a girl of principles, ideals, and refinement, from her admirer, Lyndon." (Twenty-nine years later, as President, on her birthday, he gave her a recent photograph of himself on which he had once again written those same words.) At Halloween, he returned to Texas, more certain than ever. "Let's get married," he said, "not next year, after you've done over the house, but about two weeks from now, or right away. If you say no, it just

16

proves that you don't love me enough to dare to marry me. We either do it now, or we never will."

Lady Bird, however, was confused and frightened. She was tumbling into the future too fast. How could she be sure so quickly that she was doing the right thing? What would their future be like? In one letter, she wrote, "Lyndon, please tell me as soon as you can what the deal is. I am *afraid* it is politics...I would hate for you to go into politics." She was of two minds. She wanted Lyndon to slow down his pursuit of her, which historian Michael Beschloss described as "rushing at her like a freight train." At the same time, she wanted him to catch her—in a year or so. "The only thing I knew I didn't want to do," she said, "was to say good-bye to him and put him out of my life. That much I was sure of."

She got out the Episcopal Prayer Book and read through the marriage service and asked Lyndon to do the same. Those solemn vows were not to be taken lightly, and she did not take her own life lightly.

She drove to Alabama to talk to Aunt Effie, who was sick. Her aunt discouraged the marriage as too quick, but back in Texas Lady Bird's father reminded her that Aunt Effie, though she loved Lady Bird and wanted what was best for her, also did not want her to live in Washington, over a thousand miles away. He liked Lyndon. "You've brought a lot of boys home, and this time you've brought a man," he said.

In November, Lady Bird said "yes," and before she could change her mind, Lyndon whisked her off to San Antonio to be married that very day, without telling their parents. She telephoned her friend, Cecille Harrison, to be her maid of honor, and he telephoned his friend in San Antonio, Dan Quill, to be his best man. He asked Dan not only to obtain a marriage license for them, in spite of the fact that they had not had the required doctor's exam, but also to ask the priest at St. Mark's Episcopal Church to marry them at eight o'clock that very night. Miraculously, Dan was able to do it all and also arranged for dinner afterward at the St. Anthony Hotel. When the couple arrived in San Antonio, Lady Bird and Cecille went to the hotel to dress for the wedding, and Lady Bird continued to question her own judgment. "I was getting dressed," she said, "and talking a mile a minute, still uncertain whether it would be wisest to jump out the window or go on and get married," but, "by the time the ceremony started, I was quite calm."

In the midst of such rushing about, no one thought to buy a wedding ring. This was done at the last minute at Sears Roebuck, and on November 17, 1934, Lady Bird walked down the aisle in a lavender dress, Lyndon put a $2.50 ring on her finger, and they became husband and wife.

Lady Bird Taylor, now Lady Bird Johnson, was on the threshold of the adventure of her life. You might think her education was over, but it had just begun.

1934, Lady Bird Taylor sends her photograph to Lyndon Johnson

# CHAPTER III

## First Years in Washington

The newlyweds honeymooned in Mexico for ten days, until their money ran low. They stayed in picturesque hotels, saw the gardens of Xochimilco and the pyramids in Mexico City, and Lyndon bought his bride armfuls of fresh flowers. Then they headed back to Texas to salve the hurt feelings of their families, who had been left out of the wedding. After Christmas they were off to Washington, and with their cat Poofy, they moved into a tiny one-bedroom, one-bath apartment with a foldout sofa in the living room, and Lyndon returned to his job as a congressional aide.

Lady Bird Johnson began adapting to the patterns their life together would take. The next 37 years would be thrilling, unpredictable, hectic, and draining, a tilt-a-whirl of political activity racing forward at roller coaster speed. If journalism had appealed to her in college as a way to be near the action, being married to Lyndon Johnson produced action beyond her dreams. She learned that first year that she had married a man who worked day and night, and she never knew what time he would come home for dinner. He pushed himself to the point of exhaustion and sometimes until he was sick with bronchitis or pneumonia. All their married life she would worry about his health. He moved fast and didn't

20

take time to read, so she began a habit of marking short passages in books and magazines that she thought would interest him. All home management was left to her. She had no cooking or cleaning or money-managing skills and set about to teach herself. Almost immediately they began having friends and family stay with them, sometimes for weeks and Aunt Effie sometimes for months. At times guests were sleeping both in the living room and on the screened porch.

Nine months into their married life, Lyndon called her one day and said, "How would you like to live in Austin?" To her it was as if he had asked, "How would you like to go to heaven?" President Franklin Roosevelt had recognized Lyndon as a young man of promise and wanted him to run the National Youth Administration in Texas, a new government agency designed to help train and find work for young people during the Depression, in which the unemployment rate in the United States rose to as high as 25%. For the next year and a half in Austin, Lady Bird saw little of her husband alone because he traveled the state, and when he was home in the evening, staff members crowded their house, continuing the day's work or just relaxing and playing cards until late, or even temporarily living there. Lady Bird learned how to serve meals to unexpected guests in numbers she could not predict, a pattern that continued for their entire married life. She shared the heady feeling that they were all performing a significant service to Texas young people and to their country.

Suddenly, Lyndon's career lurched in another direction. The Texas congressman from the 10th district died unexpectedly, and within 24 hours Lyndon announced his candidacy for the job. Lady Bird had grown up in a family that did not consider political office a high calling, and she had not seen elective office as the inevitable direction in which Lyndon was heading. Nevertheless, she quickly rallied and whole-heartedly financed his entry against eight older and more experienced candidates by borrowing $10,000 from her mother's estate, which her father was managing for her. In 1937 it was considered unseemly for wives to be involved in their husbands' campaigns, so Lady Bird's role was to keep Lyndon's shirts clean (he wore three or four a day) and to have dinner ready for a tired man at night. Two days before the election, he was rushed to the hospital in great pain. After an emergency appendectomy, they received news in the hospital that he was the new Texas congressman from the 10th district.

They moved back to Washington to a larger apartment, and once again they had long-term houseguests filling every extra inch of space, this time Lyndon's brother and congressional aide and the aide's wife. Lady Bird, sometimes, must have felt as if she ran a bed and breakfast. Again, Lyndon worked seven days a week, but this time Lady Bird was involved in his job. She frequently took constituents—the people who lived in the district they represented—sightseeing when they came to town, and at night she went to his office to help address letters telling Texas voters what problems in Washington he was working on. Particularly, she liked the letters sent to new high school graduates congratulating them on their achievement and offering to help them in any way they could. It was customary for congressional wives to introduce themselves by going to see the wives of other government officials (including the Cabinet, the Supreme Court, ambassadors, and other congressmen), a duty that consumed many of her days. Nights when they were not working, they often entertained their staff. They went to few Washington parties because Lyndon preferred to be with their friends from the office at dinner or playing cards or sitting on the porch watching the sun set. One party he did agree to was an invitation from President and Mrs. Roosevelt for dinner at the White House. Afterward Lady Bird wrote in her diary: "Tonight I went to my first (will it be the last and only!?!) dinner at the White House! Everything managed with a watchmaker's precision!"

In 1941 a Senate seat opened, and once again Lyndon leaped into a race against older and more experienced men. Lady Bird traveled with him, hammered posters on trees, kept his laundry clean, and made lemonade and cookies for volunteers. For the first time she made what she called "very small speeches" when he was late or unavailable for a rally. The Texas Election Bureau announced Lyndon Johnson the winner by 5,000 votes. Then, in dismay, for the next four days, they watched that win evaporate as late votes came in, and he was declared the loser by 1,311 votes. He dejectedly returned to Congress, but not for long. On December 7, 1941, the Japanese bombed Pearl Harbor in Hawaii, and the United States entered World War II. Lyndon enlisted as soon as he heard the news, and right after Christmas he left for military duty in the Pacific as a lieutenant commander.

Lady Bird was alone in Washington. She moved to a smaller apartment with her friend, Nellie Connally, to save money and rode the bus because gasoline was needed for the war effort; and, for the first time in her life, she went to work (for no pay) as manager of her husband's congressional office. This job changed her from a young, inexperienced woman into a capable, mature adult in a number of ways. It developed her managerial skills. It gave her a newfound confidence in her ability to solve difficult problems. It taught her an appreciation for the complexities of the work her husband did representing his state. It illuminated the difficulties of constituents' lives and how they might be helped. Recognizing the power of real life experience in addition to formal education, she wrote a friend that in this job she had learned more in three months than in four years of college. This was her political education.

When Lyndon returned from military service, she would add a business education to her growing resumé. With money inherited from her family, the Johnsons bought KTBC, a daytime-only, money-losing radio station with nine employees in Austin, and it became Lady Bird's full-time project. For most of 1943, she lived in Austin, grappling with its problems. She started in her usual practical way by getting on her hands and knees and scrubbing down the office's dirty floors and sweeping cobwebs off its ceiling. Then she paid the bills and hired a manager. She ran KTBC with frugality and efficiency and an eye for detail for seven months, when it made its first profit of $18. She spent the money at the dentist's. Not until 22 years later, when she became First Lady, did she give up being active in station affairs. She had, in those years, helped KTBC expand into a radio-television conglomerate affiliated with CBS. It had grown from nine to 104 employees, built its own building, and continued its profitability.

When she worked in Lyndon's Congressional office, she, like many women in World War II, learned that while men were away at war, she was capable outside of the home, and she had continued to grow that skill and confidence in the business world with KTBC.

Then, two of her dreams came true. After ten years of marriage, living in ten different apartments, the Johnsons bought a house in Washington, and Lynda, then Lucy, were born in 1944 and 1947. Their lives sped forward. Franklin Roosevelt died, and Harry S. Truman became President; America won World War II. Aunt Effie died. When Lynda Bird was four and Lucy still a baby, Lyndon once again ran for a Senate seat. Lady Bird and the children piled their belongings and themselves on a train and moved to Texas to help. For months Lady Bird led a divided life, traveling the state to campaign with her husband, which was becoming more common for women in the post-war modern world; working at the campaign headquarters; and making time for her children. A frightening event occurred the day before the election. A friend was driving her to a small-town tea to meet voters when their car skidded out of control on a rain-soaked highway and flipped over several times, landing upside down in a ditch. This was before seat belts and air bags. A shaken, sore Lady Bird crawled through the window of the car and flagged down a farmer driving by. He took them to the hospital, where, amazingly, the doctor pronounced that their injuries were not serious. Lady Bird's intent to help Lyndon win the election was serious, so she changed clothes and continued to the tea. That night, showing the stoicism characteristic of her, she met Lyndon at a political rally and didn't tell him what had happened until her darkening bruises gave her away. Instead of recuperating in bed the next day—election day—she made telephone calls all day long reminding people to go to the polls and vote. Lyndon Johnson became Texas Senator by a margin of 87 votes.

1934/1935, the newlyweds in Washington, DC

1941, Lady Bird (third from left) attends a rally in Austin
for her husband's Senate campaign

1948, Lady Bird with daughters Lucy and Lynda

# CHAPTER IV

## *The Senate and Vice-Presidential Years*

L ady Bird Johnson was 35 years old. Already she had learned many lessons that would serve her well as First Lady. She had earned college degrees in history and journalism. She had married a complex man and become his most trusted advisor. She had taught herself management of households alternating back and forth between Washington and Austin. She had run a congressional office with no prior work experience. She had overseen the growth of station KTBC as it moved into the new medium of television. She had become the mother of two adored daughters. Her life for the next 15 years as a Senator's wife and then the wife of the Vice President would continue to perfect her skills at coping with her overly busy days and overcoming her shyness.

She countered over-busyness two ways: with efficiency—always carrying a notebook on which she made and checked off to-do lists—and by stopping frequently to refresh herself and regather her energy. She walked, swam, played bridge, savored a fire in the fireplace or a vase of fresh flowers, read in bed (which she said was "sort of like eating candy"), or even ate candy—the chocolates she stashed in her bedside table. Nevertheless, trying to be both an active part of the Washington political community and of KTBC, and an involved mother to two little girls, stretched her thin. Once, when she and Lyndon were going to yet one more nighttime event, Lynda Bird complained, "Mama, Washington is made for congressmen and their wives, but it sure isn't made for their children." The Congressional Club held an annual party for the children (which Lynda and Lucy didn't like because they had to dress up and dance, and the girls had to wear white gloves), but for the most part children were not included in Washington parties. As she and Lyndon would leave the girls with a babysitter, Lady Bird always said to them, "Remember, you are loved."

Lyndon forced some of Lady Bird's shyness out of her by pushing her the way he pushed himself, always to do things she wasn't sure she was capable of, like running a radio-TV station. He encouraged her to dress up more, pay attention to her hair and clothes and makeup, which she tended to ignore, and to be more outgoing. He told her, "You don't sell for what you are worth," meaning, "You don't present yourself as the smart, accomplished woman you really are." She began to wear the bright colors he liked instead of the "mule colors" he abhorred, and she helped herself by taking both Spanish and speech lessons and practicing speaking before a mirror. Because she was ambitious to be all that she could be and was intensely curious about the world and people around her, she bravely stepped out in spite of herself

Then, in July 1955, during Lucy's eighth birthday party, Lady Bird received a telephone call saying her husband had been taken to the hospital. The news was bad. At age 46 he had suffered a heart attack. She arranged for a friend to stay with the girls, and she moved into the hospital to be with Lyndon while he fought for his life. After six weeks in the hospital, their family moved to the Texas ranch near Austin that they had bought a few years before, worried that he might not get strong enough to return to the Senate, that his political career was over. For the next frightening six months, Lady Bird devoted full-time to his recovery. She took charge in helping him to lose weight, to quit smoking, and to exercise in the swimming pool, and he did recover. He was back leading the Senate in January, and a few years later, running for Vice President on the Democratic ticket with John F. Kennedy.

By now Lady Bird was reasonably comfortable as a public speaker. She addressed women's rallies during the Presidential campaign and held an occasional press conference. Never, however, did she debate political issues. She left that to Lyndon. This was a particularly difficult period for her because her father died just weeks before the election. He did not get to see his daughter as wife of the Vice President or as First Lady of the United States.

When Kennedy won the Presidential election with Lyndon as his Vice President, Lady Bird, unknowingly, began her dress rehearsal for the role of First Lady. Their daughters were teenagers, and they had moved once again, into a large, good-for-entertaining house, The Elms. At that time the government did not furnish a house for the Vice President as it does today.

The Vice President was expected to be the eyes and ears of the President, to keep him informed about what people were thinking on important issues. Therefore, he and Lady Bird were out most nights, attending parties where they could learn people's opinions. In addition, Lady Bird stood in for Jacqueline Kennedy with frequency because the First Lady was recovering from the birth of a baby. Lady Bird's job could be called "event attendee," at women's events in the daytime and with her husband at night.

The Johnsons, in their role as "second family," also traveled the world representing the United States. Lady Bird had hardly been out of the country before, but now she covered 120,000 miles and visited 34 countries and filled notebooks with her excited impressions of new places. Especially, in each country she asked to meet "women doers" and to be taught how women conducted their lives in that country. She was keenly aware that women's roles were fast-changing, not just in our country, but throughout the world, and she would, when she became First Lady, make "women doers" a priority. After one trip to Asia, she told the press that she had been "people seeing," not "sightseeing."

Once, when the Johnsons were traveling, President and Mrs. Kennedy invited Lynda and Luci (as she now spelled her name) to a state dinner for the President of Sudan at the White House. They called their mother for advice on how to act on this formal, ceremonial occasion. In her practical way Lady Bird said, "Read all you can in the encyclopedia about the Sudan, and don't drink any of the wine at dinner."

Soon, this chapter of their lives, too, would end.

1958, the Senator's wife sits on the Capitol steps

# PART II

# *Life in the White House*

*I feel as though I am suddenly on stage for a part I never rehearsed. But like Lyndon, I will do my best. I envision my job to be balm, sustainer and sometimes critic to my husband. I want to help my children look at this job with all the reverence that is its due and to get from their unique vantage point all the knowledge that is possible. And also to help them retain the lightheartedness which every teenager is entitled to. As for my own role, it will have to emerge in deeds, not words.*

Lady Bird Johnson
In an interview on NBC News
shortly after becoming First Lady

# CHAPTER V

## *Family*

The day was Friday, November 22, 1963. The Kennedys and the Johnsons were touring Texas together to raise money for the President's upcoming re-election campaign. Already they had been to San Antonio, Houston, and Fort Worth. Now they were in Dallas. That evening the two couples intended to attend a dinner in Austin, followed by a weekend at the Johnson ranch, where already 18 freshly baked loaves of bread and 20 pecan pies covered the kitchen counters, awaiting the barbeque on the lawn Lady Bird had planned for Saturday night. The unexpected had rocked her life before. Her mother had died from a fall at home when she was a child, and her husband had suffered a severe heart attack during one of their children's birthday parties. Nothing, however, could prepare her for the shooting death of President Kennedy as he rode in an open car through the streets of Dallas on a sunny fall day. The Johnsons were following two cars behind. Shots rang out, and the President fell. Over the car radio, Lady Bird heard someone shout, "Let's get out of here," a Secret Service agent pushed Lyndon to the floor and threw his own body over him to protect him, and the two cars peeled out of the parade and sped to a nearby hospital. The Johnsons were waiting in a small room for news of the President's condition when one of President Kennedy's aides walked in and said, "He is gone." Then they knew.

Their first decision was to get back to Washington as quickly as possible to help the country face this tragedy in its national life. As they drove to the airport, Lady Bird noticed American flags already flying at half-mast, and the enormity of what had happened struck her. Once on Air Force One, before they left the ground, Lyndon Johnson was sworn in as 36th President of the United States. Then the new President and First Lady, accompanied by the former First Lady Jacqueline Kennedy, and with the body of the slain John F. Kennedy, flew to Washington, arriving after dark. Lady Bird and Lyndon got off the plane, steadying each other by holding hands, and began, in solemnity and sorrow, as President and First Lady of the United States. Lady Bird was 51 years old.

On Sunday, President and Mrs. Johnson visited the Kennedy family and then attended church. The new First Lady asked Jacqueline Kennedy to remain in the White House with her children for as long as she wanted, so it was 15 days before the Johnsons moved in. Their new home had 132 rooms and stood amid 18 acres of lawn and garden. Awed, Lady Bird said, "I walked on tiptoe and talked in a whisper." Now she was managing a household of 75 employees, including a dog-keeper and a butler. The East Wing was given over to a large staff that planned her schedule and White House parties, dealt with the 50 newspapers plus television networks that covered her activities every day, and answered the 5,000 letters she received each week. She was the first President's wife who used a press secretary. On the other side of the house—the West Wing—the President and his aides worked.

With both parents having their offices at home, the family actually saw each other more during the Presidential years than they had in the past. Lady Bird realized the strength and comfort they would all need and could give one another, and she drew them in close. Luci was 16 and Lynda 19. Lynda, a student at the University of Texas in Austin, transferred to school in Washington, accompanied by her friend from the university, Warrie Lynn Smith, who also lived with the family in the White House.

The main floor of the White House contains historic pieces of American furniture and paintings, but upstairs Lady Bird added personal touches. She decorated the girls' bedrooms, placed friends' and family photographs on the tables, Texas paintings on the walls, and needlepoint pillows depicting Texas wildflowers on the chairs. In the next years, the family quarters on the second and third floors became a center for teenage cookie baking and dances and sleepovers. If these young women had a spacious and elegant place in which to entertain their friends, they also had the media watching their every move and wanting to know why Luci had changed the spelling of her name from L-u-c-y to L-u-c-i (the press secretary's answer: "How many of you have ever been sixteen?") or why Lynda and her boyfriend had broken up. Lynda called the hovering photographers her "unfriends." The young women tried from time to time to lead the ordinary lives of non-famous teenagers by going out in dark glasses or wigs or big hats, but even if they could avoid the media, they always had two Secret Service men in dark suits close behind, even on dates.

Sometimes the girls participated in politics, particularly during the President's bid for election in 1964, when they traveled with their mother on a whistle-stop train tour

38

through the South. They both prided themselves on writing their own speeches when they campaigned. Sometimes, too, they stood in for their mother as hostesses at receptions or teas.

When she was 16, Luci was diagnosed with an eye problem that was causing her to do poorly at school in spite of her bright mind. Essentially, her eyes were not working in tandem. The doctor prescribed a series of eye exercises for her, her sight improved, and her grades at school went up dramatically. Grateful for this wonderful outcome, she began working in the doctor's office in the summers to help other youngsters with vision problems, and she became a lifelong advocate of a preschool vision-screening program called Volunteers for Vision. She was following the example her mother was setting in the War on Poverty program of helping others to have the same good fortune she enjoyed.

Meanwhile, Lynda emulated her father with an interest in history and current events. She read the newspapers and followed bills as they passed through Congress and asked her father's staff to explain legislation to her.

The President's days were long, and he didn't sleep well; Lady Bird worried about him. His best relaxation seemed to be visiting with friends over dinner, so they usually had guests in the evening. Dinner often was not until ten o'clock or later and included more talk about the problems of the day—the war in Vietnam, the struggle to make African-Americans full voting citizens, how to pass a Medicare bill. On weekends the family flew to their ranch in Texas if they could. Lady Bird also had long days and attempted to ease her own stress by swimming in the pool in the basement of the White House—frequently as many as 30 laps—or bowling in the Executive Office Building next door or watching "Gunsmoke" on television on Saturday night. Several nights a week, before the President quit work, she sat on a small blue velvet sofa in a cozy room off her bedroom, with her shoes off, looking out the window at the Washington Monument, and recording her memories of the events of her days. Years later she published these recollections in a book called *A White House Diary*.

Weddings and the arrival of grandchildren became a thrilling part of their days. Luci married first, when she was 19, the only White House bride in 50 years. Interest was so great in this event that one press reporter even requested permission to interview the President as he was walking his daughter down the aisle (permission refused). Just a year later, Lynda Bird married U.S. Marine Corps Captain Charles Robb in the East Room of the White House. Again, the press and the public cared about every small detail of this event. A week before the wedding, 500 reporters came to the White House to be briefed. One asked to know the exact number of raisins in the wedding cake (the answer: 1, 511). The day after Lynda's wedding, alone in the White House, both daughters gone, Lady Bird got out the letters the President had sent her while they were courting 33 years earlier and relived her own young romance and simpler, more private wedding.

The family's last year in the White House, 1968, was their hardest because many people in the country were angry and protesting loudly about the war in Vietnam. The United States was helping the South Vietnamese fight against the communist North Vietnamese. Many feared that each time the communists took over a country, they would become more powerful and more easily able to overwhelm the next country until, finally, all Asia would be communist. This was called the Domino Theory. Would the communists then turn to threaten those of us in the west who believed in democracy? No one knew, but others in the country, particularly young people, felt that Americans should let Asians settle their own problems rather than our risking American lives and spending American money on a war in which the risks might not be as great as we feared. Lyndon Johnson agonized. The war seemed unwinnable, but the price of endangering our own beloved democracy, unthinkable. Lynda and Luci's husbands were fighting in Vietnam, and the young women, with Luci's little boy Lyndon and Lynda's baby girl Lucinda, were living in the White House with their parents. At night, as the family tried to fall asleep, they could hear the harsh chant of protesters outside their window: "Hey, hey, LBJ, how many boys have you killed today?" Thoughts of the endangered lives of all young Americans in Vietnam, including those in their own family, haunted their days. More than ever Lady Bird tried to create a safe and soothing shelter within the house to help her family endure. Young Lyndon and Lucinda were her best allies: they lightened hearts and brought needed joy to a somber White House.

November 22, 1963, President and Mrs.
Johnson and Jacqueline Kennedy on Air Force One

1963, portrait of the family in the White House

1967, the First Lady pushes her grandson,
Patrick Lyndon Nugent, in a baby carriage behind the White House

1965, the best relaxation is at the LBJ Ranch in Texas

# CHAPTER VI

## *Busy Days*

N o two days were alike. Lady Bird's unending array of activities included traveling frequently—flying to Greece to represent the United States at the funeral of King Paul, giving a graduation address at Radcliffe College, listening to her husband make nine speeches in nine Midwest towns in one day. In Australia she stayed in the home of the Prime Minister and his wife and met their well-mannered pet kangaroo in their living room. In Korea she heard "The Yellow Rose of Texas" played in her honor. She swam in the Gulf of Siam and snorkeled in the Caribbean. She traveled 200,000 miles in her five years in the White House, or the equivalent of eight times around the world. Her lifelong hunger to experience the world was well fed.

One memorable trip, dubbed the Whistle-Stop, occurred in 1964, when she felt compelled to soldier into the middle of a momentous political battle in spite of the fact that she preferred to leave politics to the President. Lyndon Johnson was bringing civil rights change to a white South that wanted its traditional segregation between whites and blacks to remain as it had been since the founding of the country. Many Southerners feared their lives would be disrupted in ways they could not imagine by too much change too fast, if segregation ended and more blacks voted and participated in political life. President Johnson knew that if the South did not change, it would become an economic backwater, and morally he knew it was wrong for blacks to be denied opportunities that whites took for granted. Some issues were important symbolically, like whether African-Americans could sit at the front of a public bus instead of only at the rear, and some had very real consequences, like whether a black student could register at a Southern university that previously had been open only to white students.

Lady Bird agreed with her husband. Yet she grieved for this turmoil in her own part of the country. Her family was from Alabama, and she had grown up in Texas. When the President ran for election in 1964, she suggested she travel to the South and campaign as one Southerner talking to other Southerners and quelling their fears. "We must go," she said. "We must let them know that we love the South. We respect them. We have not turned our backs on them."

The plan was daring; no First Lady before her had ever campaigned independently of her husband. How would she be treated when she talked about emotionally charged issues? Could her soft Southern manner calm overwrought people, or would they consider her a traitor to her own? She decided she had to try. She and her staff put together a train trip, which they called a whistle-stop because in each town the train would whistle its arrival, stop long enough for her to make a speech standing on the back of the caboose, and then pull away, headed for the next town.

One day Lady Bird sat down at her desk and for 11 straight hours called Southern governors, senators, and congressmen and said she was coming to their state, and would they meet the train and stand beside her? A few proudly said yes, some reluctantly agreed to be there, and some begged off with flimsy excuses. A plan was made. Nineteen train cars carrying over 200 reporters would accompany her on a train called "The Lady Bird Express." It would make 47 stops in eight states over a four-day period, and in each she would make a speech from the back of the train. "Don't give me the easy towns," she said. "Let me take the tough ones."

At each stop the reporters clamored off the train, watched Mrs. Johnson along with the audience, took pictures and wrote stories, rushed to the temporary telephones set up for them to call the stories in to their newspapers, and when they heard two loud toots of the train whistle, piled back on board and headed for the next stop. Sometimes there were as many as 13 stops in a day. The White House office warned the reporters before they left to wear tennis shoes. On the train they were served Southern foods—beaten biscuits and ham, hush puppies, grits, black-eyed peas. Lady Bird wanted the press to love the South also.

Much of the trip was a success. Huge crowds formed along the tracks in the countryside just to watch her go by, and thousands came out in the towns where she stopped to speak. She received so many bouquets of flowers that the train could not hold them, so several times she asked the police in a town to pick them up and deliver them to nearby hospitals for patients to enjoy. At one stop a woman shouted to her, "I got up at three o'clock this morning and milked 20 cows so I could come to see you, Lady Bird." Lady Bird blew her a kiss.

Other moments were unsettling and required all her mettle to face. She heard rumors of a sniper and of a bomb on the track. She saw signs saying, "Lady Bird, Lady Bird, Fly Away," or "Blackbird Go Home," and crowds booed her. At one stop, hecklers beat drums and chanted, "We want Barry, we want Barry" (Barry Goldwater was the President's Republican opponent). Lady Bird raised her hand to quiet them and said clearly to all assembled, "My friends, in this country we are entitled to many viewpoints. You are entitled to yours. But right now, I'm entitled to mine." Her soft voice and steely willingness to stand behind her words quieted them, and they listened.

The message she delivered at each stop was this: "We must search for the ties that bind us together, not settle for the tensions that tend to divide us."

Arriving back in Washington at the end of the four days, Lady Bird called them the "four most dramatic days of my political life." She had done her job well.

When she was not traveling, often she was entertaining—one day producing a country fair on the lawn of the White House for children of congressmen and government officials, complete with Ferris wheel and cotton candy and a fortune teller; on another day inviting astronauts and their families to spend the night at the White House; and on another, welcoming historians who had written about Abraham Lincoln and actors who had played him to a Lincoln birthday party, where she decorated the tables with Lincoln's own china and took the guests in buses to see the Lincoln Memorial. Sometimes the staff was still tidying up from one party as guests were arriving for another. Of all the glittering events, however, nothing compared to the magic of state dinners.

A state dinner is a party honoring the head of another country and is a useful tool in United States relations with foreign nations. Lady Bird took great care to make these events memorable for the honorees and for the other guests, many of whom came from different parts of the United States and had never been to the White House before. The Johnsons' first state dinner was for President Antonio Segni of Italy and Signora Segni. The afternoon of the dinner, in her thorough way, she sat down and read about Italy so she could talk intelligently to President and Signora Segni about their country. She studied the guest list, which included every member of Congress of Italian descent, the President's Italian barber, and Italian-Americans of accomplishment from throughout the United States. She wanted to be able to make each one feel personally welcomed. She looked at photographs of those traveling with the Segnis so she could call them by name. When the Segni's limousine drove up to the White House, President and Mrs. Johnson met them outside in spite of icy weather and snow on the ground. In the second-floor family quarters, the two couples exchanged gifts, as was customary. The Johnsons chose for President Segni a silver box for his desk with the words of 19th century American poet Henry Wadsworth Longfellow engraved on it: "Italy remains to all the land of dreams and visions of delight." Meanwhile, the other guests talked to each other on the main floor and waited in black tie and long dresses for the arrival of the Presidents and their wives. A military band played "Hail to the Chief" as the two couples ceremoniously descended the grand staircase and formed a receiving line to have a few words with each of the 140 guests. Then the Johnsons led the way into the flower-filled dining room, which was large enough to seat everyone, and where the two Presidents raised their glasses in toast to each other. Filet of beef was the main course. Coffee was served after dinner in another room, followed by entertainment in a third room, where a temporary stage and small gold chairs for everyone to sit on had been set up. Mrs. Johnson introduced the program: Robert Merrill, star of the Metropolitan Opera in New York, singing Italian arias. In addition to her desire to show appreciation for the Italians' love of opera, she wanted the Segnis to enjoy something American, so a group of young people called the New Christy Minstrels played and sang American folk songs, including "When the Saints Go Marching In." Their music, which was wildly popular with teenagers, wafted upstairs, and Luci, who was studying for exams, came down to listen with the adults. Italian opera and American hootenanny could not have been in greater contrast, nor could the guests have been more pleased. One could sway to the arias and tap one's foot to the folk tunes.

Through many state dinners, Mrs. Johnson developed her style. Even though the groups were large, she wanted to be sure to have at least a few moments of contact with each guest. She wrote in her diary: "If it is 'small town' to try to make every guest at a party feel at ease and have a good time, then I'll cheerfully be labeled 'small town'! I have been to some elegant, sophisticated parties that were also cold and tiresome. I don't want that sort of entertaining in my time here." She had guests sit at companionable round tables for ten rather than at a long and formal banquet table. She asked friends to serve as hosts at each table to introduce strangers and to stimulate conversation. If a guest came alone, a Marine officer in dress uniform escorted that person around the room introducing him or her during the pre-dinner reception. (This was the assignment Chuck Robb had when he met Lynda Bird.) After dinner, while everyone was still sitting in the dining room, a group of 20 violinists from the U. S. Army swept through the room playing romantic music, and this marked the end of the meal and time to move to the next room. Sometimes, instead of entertainment, there was dancing, which she and the President both loved. Sometimes she whispered in his ear the name of a guest she thought he should dance with. Invariably, guests left exhilarated by their once-in-a-lifetime experience at a state dinner in the White House.

1966, President and Mrs. Johnson in Honolulu

1964 Lady Bird campaigns from the back of a train on the Whistle-Stop Tour through the South

Lady Bird Johnson and Tiffany & Co. collaborate to create a set of china for the White House, picturing the wildflowers of America

## CHAPTER VII

# *Accomplishments*

Lady Bird involved herself in every issue important to her husband, and, in addition, she chose four areas about which she felt a passion and made a difference by her efforts. These were White House preservation, the War on Poverty, "Women Doers," and, most importantly, the environment.

### White House Preservation

She recognized that the White House, in addition to being the First Family's home, was a museum belonging to the American people, full of historic furniture and memories of former Presidential families. It welcomed thousands of visitors a year. With a group called the Committee for the Preservation of the White House, she began adding American art to the important furniture collection started by Jacqueline Kennedy. Now, thanks to Lady Bird Johnson, donations of paintings by definitive American artists hang throughout the White House, including Winslow Homer, Thomas Eakins, Robert Henri, Mary Cassatt, Thomas Sully, and Maurice Prendergast. She also oversaw the care of this museum, doing necessary jobs, like replacing shredded drapes in the State Dining Room, and creative projects like consulting with Tiffany & Co. to design a new china for state dinners with an

American eagle in the center of each piece and the American wildflowers she so loved bordering the edges.

## War on Poverty

Lyndon Johnson hated poverty from the time, as a young man, he taught poor children in South Texas. He saw that when they came to school hungry, when they had no medical care, and when their parents could not read to them or send them to nursery school or kindergarten, they simply could not keep up with more fortunate children. One of his first acts as President was to declare a War on Poverty. Lady Bird immediately enlisted in his cause. She became honorary chairman of a pre-school program called Head Start, which appealed to her because, as she wrote in her Diary, "it has such *hope.*" The program began small, with 100,000 underprivileged five- and six-year-olds going to school for eight weeks in the summer before they started first grade. They had a medical examination, one good free meal a day, and simple lessons in manners and vocabulary improvement. Many had never seen a pencil before and did not know that a banana should be peeled before eating. "They have been stranded on an island of nothingness," she said. "Some don't know even a hundred words because they have not heard a hundred words." She saw how she could help to bring public attention to their crying need and its remedy by visiting Head Start programs around the country, which she did, with busloads of reporters alongside her. She continued to support and speak out for Head Start programs after she left the White House.

## Women Doers

Lady Bird was proud of women. She wanted their accomplishments recognized, and she wanted women to encourage one another by meeting together to discuss substantive problems. She held 16 Women Doers lunches, to which she invited women from throughout the country to come to the White House to hear and talk with a woman who was an expert in a particular field. The speeches covered a broad range of subjects, from the space program to city planning. One, entitled "Crime and What the Average Citizen Can Do to Stop It," made clear how complex, interrelated, and emotion-packed were the problems of the 1960s. After three speakers told the group the helpful ways their communities were dealing with crime in the streets, well-known entertainer Eartha Kitt stood before the 50 guests, pointed her finger at the First Lady, and in impassioned voice, said, "You send the best of this country off to be shot and maimed. No wonder the kids rebel and take pot. They don't want to go to school because they're going to be snatched off from their mothers to be shot in Vietnam." Stunned, Mrs. Johnson told herself to be calm, then replied, "Because there is a war...that still doesn't give us a free ticket not to try to work for better things—against crime in the streets, and for better education and better health for our people..." Thunderous applause followed, and the discussion broadened from there into the thorniest issues of the day—poverty, crime, war, and racism—and the women stayed until four o'clock in the afternoon in animated discussion. As always, the First Lady tried to hear out the anger and to search out solutions. This event made national news, and 35,000 letters poured into the White House with suggestions for fighting crime from women throughout the country.

**Environment**

Lady Bird had found adventure and solace and deep-felt beauty in the outdoors since she was a small child. She thrilled equally to a rugged raft trip in the wilderness and to the first Texas bluebonnets popping out in March. It was natural that she would choose the environment as the primary focus of her years in the White House. As she explained it, "Shortly after the inauguration in January of '65, I knew I wanted to concentrate whatever I could do on whatever parts of Lyndon's program that made my heart sing, that came naturally, that belonged to me....All my life, nature, scenery, the beauties of this country had been my joy, what fueled my spirit, made me happy. Lyndon made a speech...and a great deal of it was about the environment, about conservation. I decided that's for me."

Her extensive work on behalf of the environment was dubbed her beautification program. Beautification was a word she did not like but one that stuck in people's minds. To her the word seemed "trivial" and "prissy." She had much more in mind than making the countryside pretty. She wanted to protect the land for our children so that they had clean water and air and seashores and parklands to walk and play in. Up until that time, Americans had not thought much about how their pesticides and automobile exhausts and the things they threw on the ground were damaging the land, and many people did not know about some of our more remote national parks until Lady Bird brought these things to their attention by taking reporters to places like Snake River in Grand Teton National Park and Big Bend in West Texas. "Call it corny, if you will," she said, "but I want to boast about America." Sometimes they were hiking through the wilderness, alert for rattlesnakes or bears; sometimes they were singing songs around a camp fire; one time they had to fly twice over a landing strip to shoo away a herd of antelope. She took nine of these trips, and the articles in the press about them produced results. If she visited a national park, the tourist numbers tripled within a week. After she hosted foreign correspondents, articles about the wonders of touring the United States appeared all over Europe. She knew she was successfully teaching Americans to be proud of their natural beauty when, in Praha, Texas, a little boy pressed a dollar bill, folded many times, into her hand and said, "This is for your beautification project."

She worked hard on a bill before Congress that would clean up the clutter of our highways by limiting billboards and junkyards along their edges. She even visited congressmen's offices to ask for their support, a rare thing for a First Lady to do. The bill would not have passed without her efforts, and for that reason, everyone called it the Lady Bird Bill. On the day he signed the bill into law, the President held a ceremony in the East Room of the White House in which he signed the bill, then handed the fountain pen to Lady Bird and kissed her on the cheek in congratulation.

She set out to make Washington, D. C. more beautiful and more livable in hopes that cities all around the country would see how they could do the same. Looking to the future, she told the mayor of Austin that she hoped to work on a beautification project there when they retired. She felt that environmental beauty must not be limited to the wilderness, but should be a part of our daily living as we maneuver through our cities, where most of us are most of the time. One friend gave her 800,000 daffodil bulbs to plant, and they are still blooming in Washington today. When she planted 50 dogwood trees along the Potomac River, one for each state, she invited governors' wives from throughout the country to accompany her. Each one would throw in a spadeful of dirt on her own state's tree simultaneously, with the Navy Band playing and flags of every state flying. The weather did not cooperate. The governors' wives had to step in mud up to their shoe-tops to plant their trees; the wind blew hard, and the temperature was a teeth-chattering 29 degrees. The women all had to wash mud off their shoes before they could go to lunch. Worst of all, very few of the media braved the weather to cover the event. Those trees, too, continue to bloom in Washington each spring.

With her interests in both the environment and the poverty program, she found a way to combine the two. First she drove around Washington looking for run-down sites in poor neighborhoods. She wanted the people who lived there to be able to take pride in their surroundings. Through gifts from friends, she was able to landscape many schools and to add playground equipment and to persuade school principals to keep those playgrounds open after school.

One environmental effort produced a little unplanned drama. Lassie, the collie of TV fame, came to the White House to launch a campaign to keep the national forests clean by picking up litter. In a ceremony in the East Garden outside the White House, Lassie carried a bouquet of flowers between his teeth and presented them to Mrs. Johnson (in spite of the name, Lassie was a male dog). Then he picked up some scraps of paper tossed on the ground and dropped them in a trashcan just as his trainer had taught him. More than forty photographers and seventy reporters recorded the event while television cameras rolled. Suddenly, the Johnsons' own collie Blanco, known to be temperamental, appeared, growling at Lassie and looking for a fight. A few tense moments passed as the dogs circled each other threateningly, before a White House employee saved the day by grabbing Blanco and getting him away from his TV star competitor.

In 1968, just before the Johnsons left office, the U.S. Department of the Interior, which is the government agency responsible for protecting the environment, named an island in the Potomac River Lady Bird Johnson Park in appreciation for her monumental efforts to conserve and enhance America's land.

1968, the First Lady visits a Head Start classroom

1968, Mrs. Johnson walks among the Giant Redwoods in California

1967, Lassie helps with the Keep America Beautiful campaign

1956, President Lyndon Johnson hands the pen with which he has just
signed the Highway Beautification Act to his wife,
who was responsible for its passage

# PART III

# *Life After the White House*

*Claudia Alta Taylor—Lady Bird Johnson—served the beauty in nature and the beauty in us—and right down to the end of her long and bountiful life, she inspired us to serve them, too.*

Bill Moyers
former Press Secretary to Lyndon Johnson
speaking at Lady Bird Johnson's funeral

# CHAPTER VIII

## *Leaving the White House*

In 1968 Lady Bird and Lyndon had to make a momentous decision for the country and for themselves. Should he run for re-election? Everyone in America hated the Vietnam War, but they were at odds with one another about whether the country should continue fighting to defeat communism or whether they should leave the field to save American lives. The President feared he had done all he could to bring Americans together on this all-important question, and now, perhaps a fresh voice was needed to unite them. He believed that a hard-fought campaign might tear the country apart. Yet he had more he wanted to achieve for his country, and he found it hard to imagine turning away from its distress. Lady Bird so dreaded more bitter division in the country with him at its center that she wrote in her diary, "I face the prospect of another campaign like an open-ended stay in a concentration camp." Lady Bird would support her husband whatever he decided, but she knew how exhausted he was and how troubled by the country's problems, and she could not help but want him to have some relief from the strain and some years of enjoying his family and his ranch. She wrote him a nine-page memo laying out the pros and cons of his retiring, and the two of them discussed it privately for months. When the

President went on the air to address the nation on March 31, he still was not sure what his decision would be. He decided during his address and ended his speech by saying, "...I have concluded I should not permit the Presidency to become involved in the partisan divisions that are developing in this political year. With America's sons in the field far away, with America's future under challenge here at home, with our hopes and the world's hopes for peace in the balance every day, I do not believe that I should devote an hour or a day of my time to any personal partisan causes or any duties other than the awesome duties of this office, the Presidency of your country. Accordingly, I will not seek, and I will not accept the nomination of my party for another term as your President."

All America gasped.

# CHAPTER IX

## *The First Years of Retirement*

On January 20, 1969, Lady Bird and Lyndon, with their white dog Yuki, greeted Pat and Richard Nixon and their poodle Vicky and terrier Pasha as they drove up to the White House in a black limousine. Inside the mansion, 24-year-old Lynda and 21-year-old Luci began filling in Tricia, 22, and Julie, 20, on what they would find it like to be First Children. Then the Johnsons left the White House for the last time. As they walked out the door, Lady Bird whispered in her husband's ear, "I have no regrets." By nightfall, America had inaugurated a new President, and the Johnson family was sitting by a welcoming fire at their Texas ranch, home to stay after 34 years in Washington.

In the four years left of their life together, the Johnsons oversaw the final construction of the Lyndon B. Johnson Library and Museum on the University of Texas campus in Austin. Actually, Lady Bird had been working on this project since early in her husband's administration, when the University of Texas proposed that the President house the papers relating to his long political career in a building on their campus and that there also be a school of public affairs to be named after him. The President had assigned Lady Bird the job of planning such a building. She traveled to the Truman,

Eisenhower, and Roosevelt Libraries to see what had been done before and came away from her study seeing the value of its being more than just a warehouse for her husband's 45 million papers. She wanted it to be a visual museum with displays that brought to life the country's history for the tourist. And, importantly, she saw it as a place for experts to come together to discuss the problems of the day. The LBJ Library opened in May of 1971 with bands playing and 3,000 people in attendance to hear President Richard Nixon speak and to eat barbeque on the lawn. The Library became the focal point of the Johnsons' new life in Texas, and it was there that the President made his last public appearance at a symposium of Civil Rights leaders from around the country. In a tired, solemn voice, just a month before his death, he urged Americans to continue their progress in making equal rights a reality for all Americans. Then, on January 22, 1973, Lyndon Johnson had the heart attack that ended his life. Lady Bird would live another 34 years alone, years as full of accomplishment as those before.

1968, the Johnsons retire to their Texas ranch

Lady Bird Johnson suggests the red archival boxes with gold
Presidential seals, which are a stunning feature of the
LBJ Library and Museum in Austin, Texas

# CHAPTER X

## *The Last Years Alone*

Lady Bird had been married 37 years. For the next 34 years, she continued to discover the world and contribute to it with the same zest and sense of purpose she had displayed as First Lady. She did not recognize retirement to be an option, and as a widow, she led a second life as full as the one before.

Now grandchildren—seven of them—brought a new dimension to her days. Known to them as "Nini," she tried to accommodate each one's interests. She swam with them at the ranch, cheered them at sporting events, contributed to the charities they cared about, and traveled on individual trips with each one—to Africa, Alaska, Morocco, but mostly to Western Europe. She lived also to know ten great-grandchildren and even got to go to one's kindergarten class to read to the students, just as she had done so many years before with Head Start.

She continued helping the LBJ Library and the School of Public Affairs to thrive as places to think about history and politics and to talk about the country's problems. Today about 400 students attend the LBJ School of Public Affairs, and in the Library historians and students study in the reading room while tourists view LBJ's career and the history of the country laid out before them in exhibits that, through the years, have included everything from the costumes astronauts wore to walk on the moon to General Cornwallis' letter of surrender in the American Revolution to the Declaration of Independence. Presidents and First Ladies and Supreme Court justices and the Queen of England and actors and college professors and television newscasters and a former ruler of Russia and historians and politicians have appeared on its stage, and the discussion has been rich. Traditionally, when a guest spoke, Lady Bird sat on the front row of the auditorium to hear the program and continued conversation afterward with the speaker at dinner on the top floor of the Library. She was both their hostess and most avid listener, never losing that eagerness to learn that typified her.

Additionally, she did for Austin what she had done earlier for Washington, DC: she made it more beautiful and more livable. Some years before, the city had dammed a portion of the Colorado River to form Town Lake in the downtown area, but over time the lake had become polluted and choked with weeds. The Austin City Council formed the Town Lake Beautification Committee with Lady Bird as its honorary chair. Using the same ceremonial spade with which she had introduced the country to beautification in Washington, she kicked off the campaign by planting flowering trees to announce that beautification had begun. For five years she oversaw the planting of trees and flowers and the laying out of hike and bike trails, and she raised money from the community until, today, Town Lake is the centerpiece of Austin. People can walk or bike over ten miles of trails, watch college rowers train on the lake, fish from the shore, admire ducks and geese and swans and songbirds, see the seasons change and the sun set, paddle their own boats in the clean waters—

75

all in the middle of a big city. At the time the trail was being created, the Austin City Council asked to change the name from Town Lake to Lady Bird Lake, but she said, "No."

She tried to limit her activities to those she most cared about, but found herself overscheduled nevertheless. Of the many groups that clamored for her service as a member of their governing boards, she chose two that addressed her particular loves: the governing board of the University of Texas, called the Board of Regents, and the National Geographic Society. In addition, she again involved herself with business matters at the television and radio station KTBC. As if that were not enough, she took on one last monumental venture.

At a ceremony for her 70th birthday she scattered bluebonnet seeds, a high school band played "America the Beautiful," and she announced that she intended to spend the rest of her life studying wildflowers, which she called her "forever" project. She began by giving 60 acres and $125,000 for the founding of the National Wildflower Research Center. The purpose of the Center was to study the use of native flowers and plants, first in Texas, and then across the country, as a way both to beautify our surroundings and to maintain parks and highways and lawns at the lowest possible cost. No one else had come up with such an idea. It was, she said, "my way of paying rent for the space I have taken up in this highly interesting world." Today, renamed The Lady Bird Johnson Wildflower Center, it has grown from 60 to 279 acres and has been incorporated into the University of Texas at Austin, where scientists and students study the more than 650 plant species growing on its grounds. Lady Bird Johnson first introduced environmentalism as a national priority in the 1960s, and with the founding of the Wildflower Center, ensured that it will remain a part of the national conversation.

The last years of Lady Bird Johnson's life presented her with one last enormous challenge: how to live joyfully in the face of failing health. Determined not to miss any of the adventures of life still available to her, she did what she had always done: she found ways to make the best of her situation. When her sight deteriorated, she used a magnifying glass to see wildflowers and listened to the books she could no longer read. Her children and grandchildren read to her, and one of her great grandchildren even read her *Little House on the Prairie.* When she could no longer walk, Lynda and Luci pushed her in a wheelchair down the hike and bike trail that she had created along Town Lake. When a stroke took away her voice, she communicated by writing on a small pad that she kept close by. Her hearing and her curiosity never left her, and she found pleasure in listening to others' conversation, responding with smiles and nods and claps of her hands to what they said so that they understood what she was thinking even though she could no longer tell them in words.

Finally, her long life of 94 years ended on Wednesday, July 11, 2007. That night the University of Texas 27-story tower shone bright orange from top to bottom in her honor. Until after midnight, thousands of people flocked to the nearby LBJ Library, where her body lay in repose. At her funeral in Austin on Saturday, First Lady Laura Bush, four former First Ladies, and two former Presidents sat together behind the family. One speaker, Lucinda Robb, characterized her grandmother as "the most quietly confident, least needy person I ever knew. She didn't need you to do anything for her. She had such a light touch." The next day, Sunday, a motorcade carried her home to the family cemetery at the ranch with more thousands lining the route, many holding wildflowers or waving flags. There she was laid to rest under the live oak trees next to her husband, who had died 34 years earlier.

Within a few days the Austin City Council proclaimed that from now on Town Lake would be called Lady Bird Lake, a most fitting tribute to our Environmental First Lady, a real "women's doer," who spent a lifetime making the world a welcoming place for all people.

1981, Mrs. Johnson attends an LBJ Foundation meeting in Austin

2000, Lady Bird with Luci and Lynda

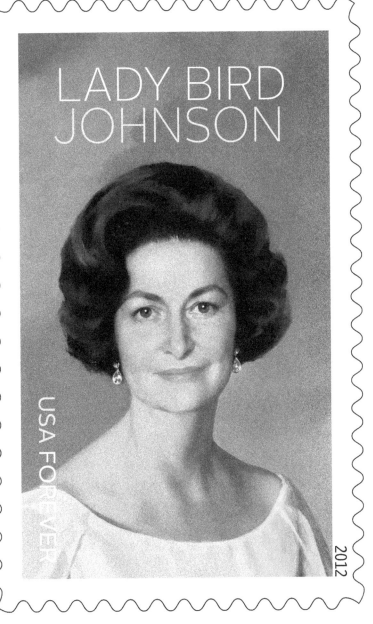

LADY BIRD
JOHNSON

USA FOREVER

2012

2012, the U.S. Postal Service issues a stamp in memory
of Lady Bird Johnson

# Selected Bibliography & Recommended Reading List

Lady Bird Johnson's own words tell her life best. They can be read in

Johnson, Lady Bird, *A White House Diary*, University of Texas Press, Austin, 2007

Gillette, Michael L., *Lady Bird Johnson: an Oral History*, Oxford University Press, 2012

Updegrove, Mark, *Indomitable Will*, Crown, 2012

For a thorough look at her work with the environment, read

Gould, Louis, *Lady Bird Johnson and the Environment*, University Press of Kansas, 1988

An entertaining description of life in the White House, written by her press secretary, is

Carpenter, Liz, *Ruffles and Flourishes*, Doubleday & Company, Inc., Garden City, N. Y., 1969

Good general biographies from childhood through the White House years, include

Montgomery, Ruth, *Mrs. LBJ*, Holt, Reinhart and Winston, 1964

Smith, Marie, *The President's Lady: An Intimate Biography of Mrs. Lyndon B. Johnson*, Random House, New York, 1964

A book published in tribute to Lady Bird Johnson on her 80th birthday, including tributes from her friends around the world, is

Middleton, Harry, *Lady Bird Johnson: A Life Well Lived*, The Lyndon Baines Johnson Foundation, Austin, Texas, 1992

CPSIA information can be obtained
at www.ICGtesting.com
Printed in the USA
FSHW04n1739230418
47346FS

9 781457 524097